Ricky Roogle

HOW TO DRAW SKINS
for Am@ng.us Fans

AF175252

NOT AN OFFICIAL INNERSLOTH PRODUCT. NOT APPROVED BY OR ASSOCIATED WITH INNERSLOTH.

Bibliografische Information der Deutschen Nationalbibliothek:
Die Deutsche Nationalbibliothek verzeichnet diese Publikation in der Deutschen Nationalbibliografie; detaillierte bibliografische Daten sind im Internet über http://dnb.dnb.de abrufbar.

© 2021 Ricky Roogle; 1. Auflage
Covergraphic, text & illustrations © 2021 Ricky Roogle
contact author: ricky.roogle@t-online.de

Herstellung und Verlag: BoD – Books on Demand, Norderstedt
ISBN: 9783752658743

Space for your drawing

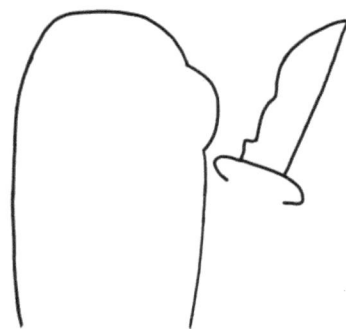

Step 1: We start with the outline of the knife and the body without legs

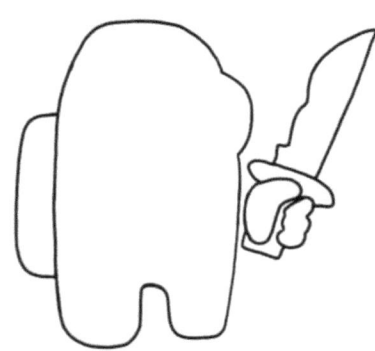

Step 2: We finish drawing the body with legs and hand

Step 3: We draw the visor and the oxygen tank and further details

Space for your drawing

Step 1: We start with the outline of the banana and the body without legs

Step 2: We finish drawing the body and complete the visor, the banana and start with the clothes

Step 3: We draw the oxygen tank and further details

Space for your drawing

Step 1: We start with the outline of the helmet and the body without legs

Step 2: We finish the body, draw the oxygen tank and visor and complete the helmet

Step 3: We complete the drawing with further details

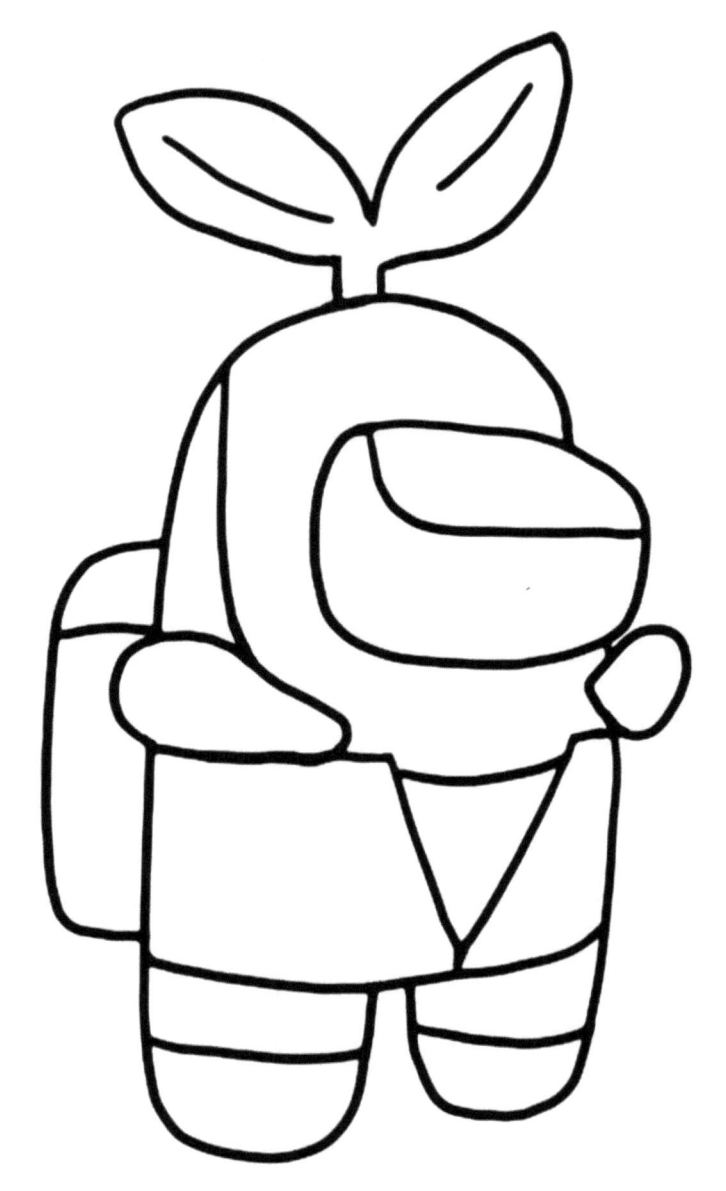

Step 1: We start with the outline of the plant hat and the body without legs

Step 2: We finish drawing the body, draw the visor and start with the clothes

Step 3: We draw the oxygen tank and complete all further details

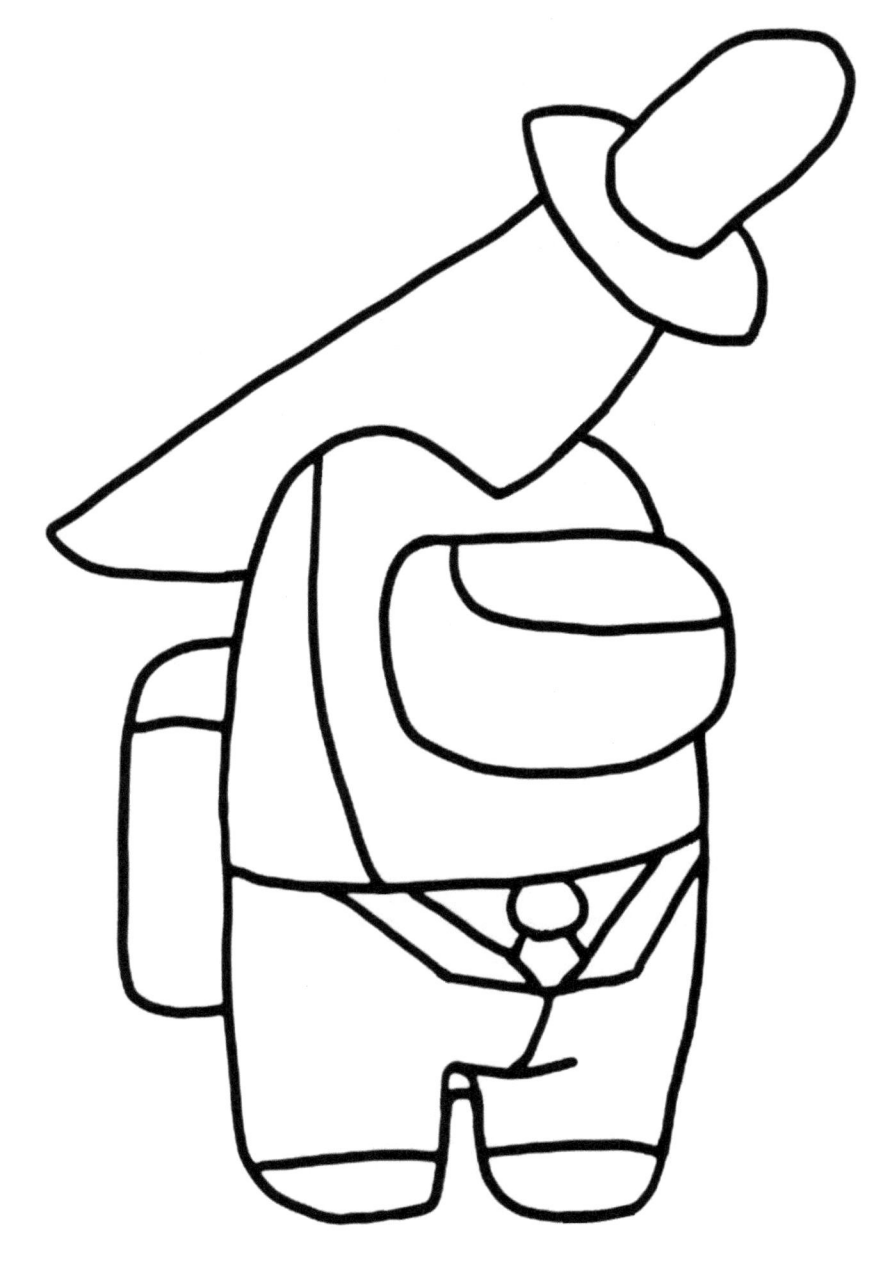

Space for your drawing

Step 1: We start with the outline of the sword and the body without legs

Step 2: We finish drawing the body, draw the oxygen tank, the visor and complete the sword

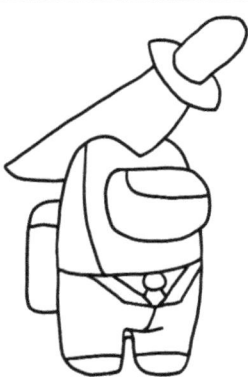

Step 3: We complete the drawing with clothes and further details

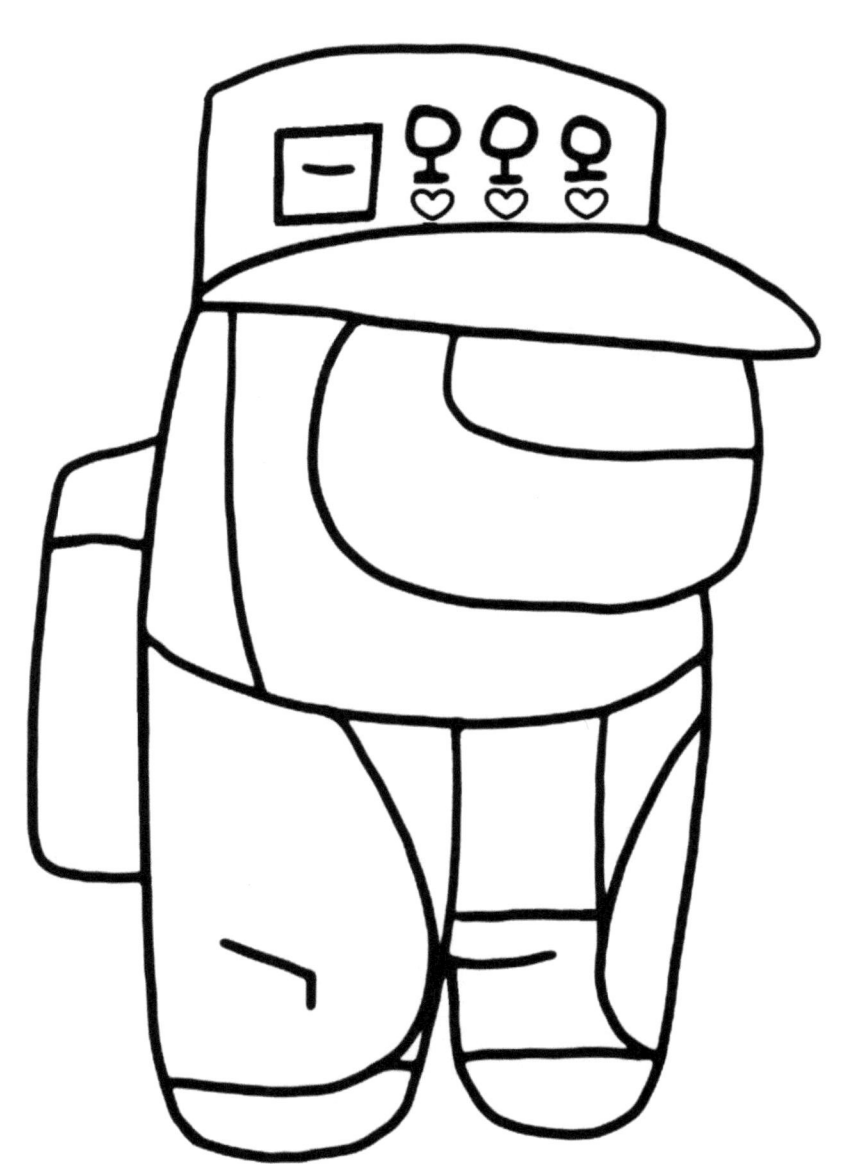

Space for your drawing

Step 1: We start with the outline of the hat and the body without legs

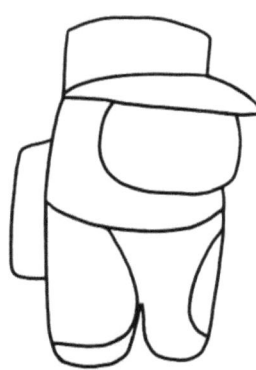

Step 2: We finish drawing the body, draw the oxygen tank, the visor and start with the clothes

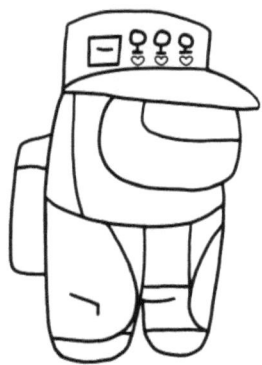

Step 3: We complete the drawing with further details

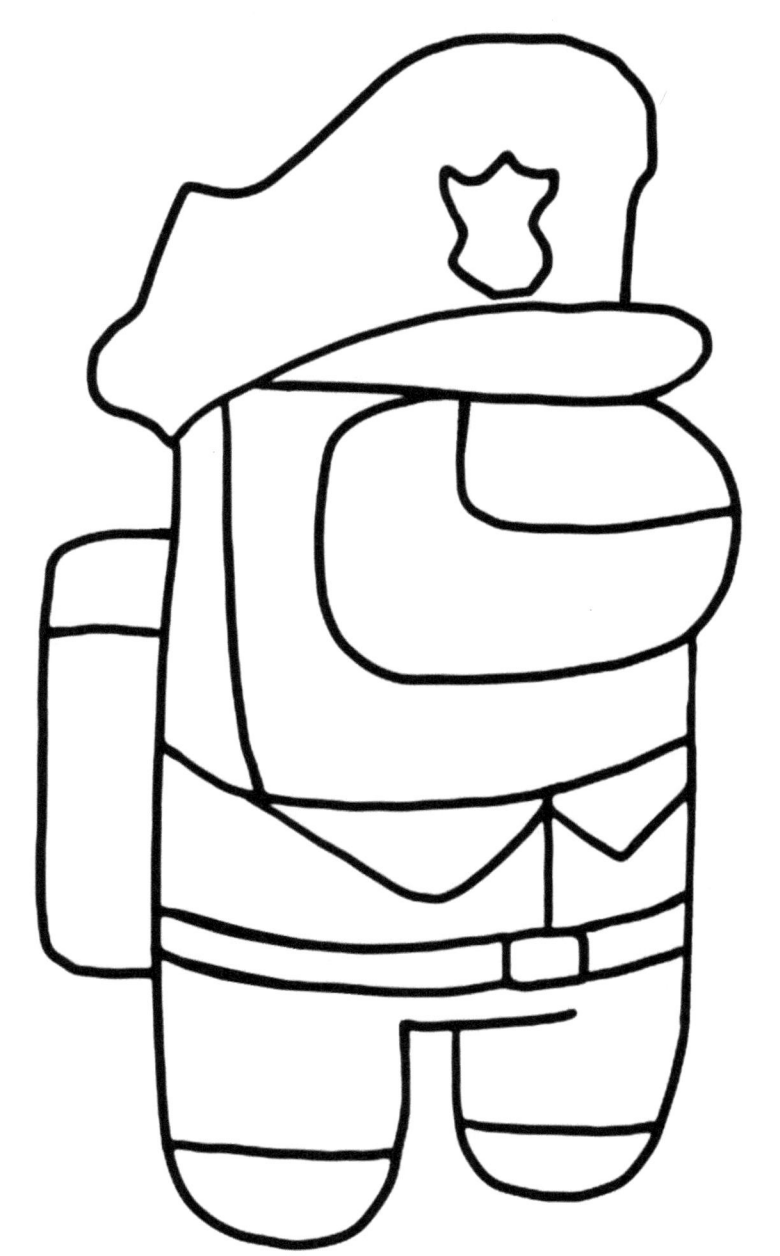

Space for your drawing

Step 1: We start with the outline of the hat and the body without legs

Step 2: We finish drawing the body, draw the oxygen tank, the visor and start with the clothes

Step 3: We complete the drawing with further details

Step 1: We start with the outline of the hat and the body without legs

Step 2: We finish drawing the body, drawing the oxygen tank, the visor and start with the clothes

Step 3: We complete the drawing with further details

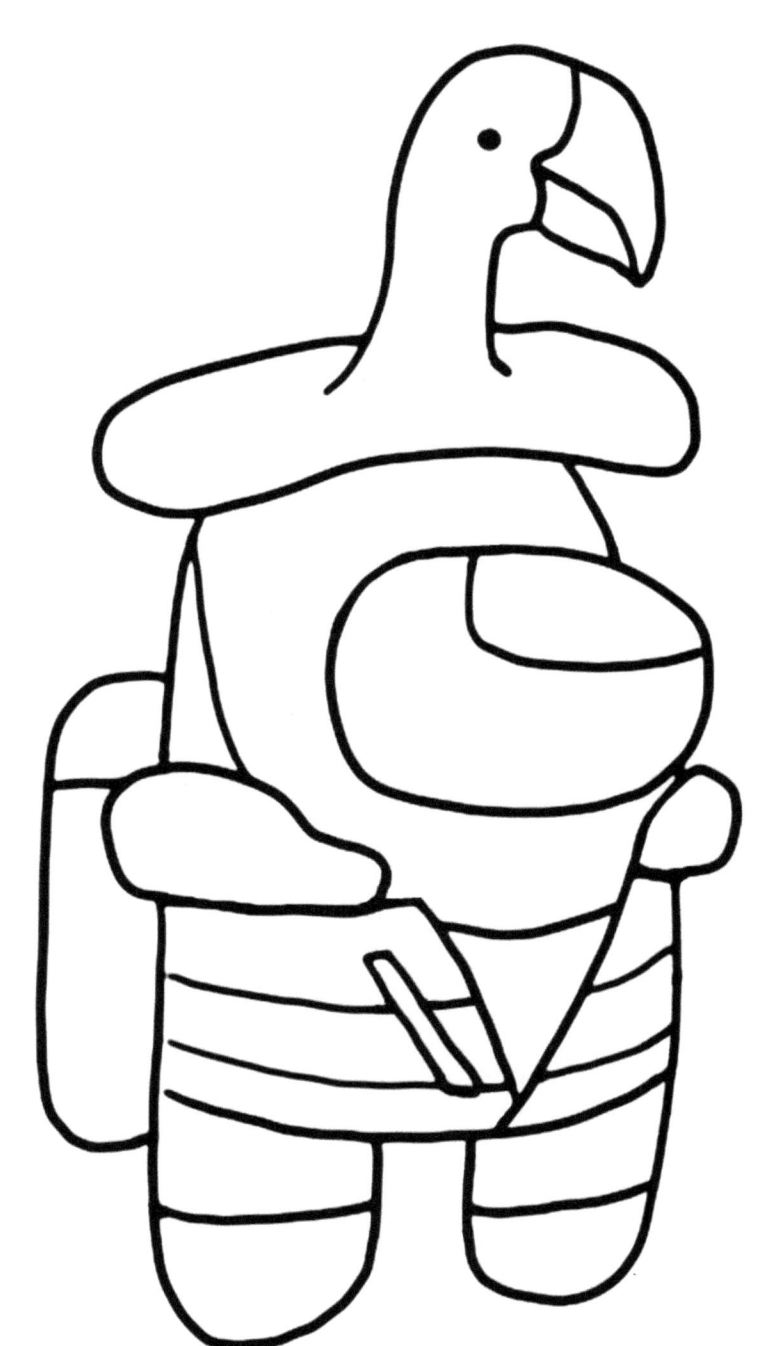

Step 1: We start with the outline of the hat and the body without legs

Step 2: We finish drawing the body, drawing the oxygen tank, the visor and start with the clothes

Step 3: We complete the drawing with further details

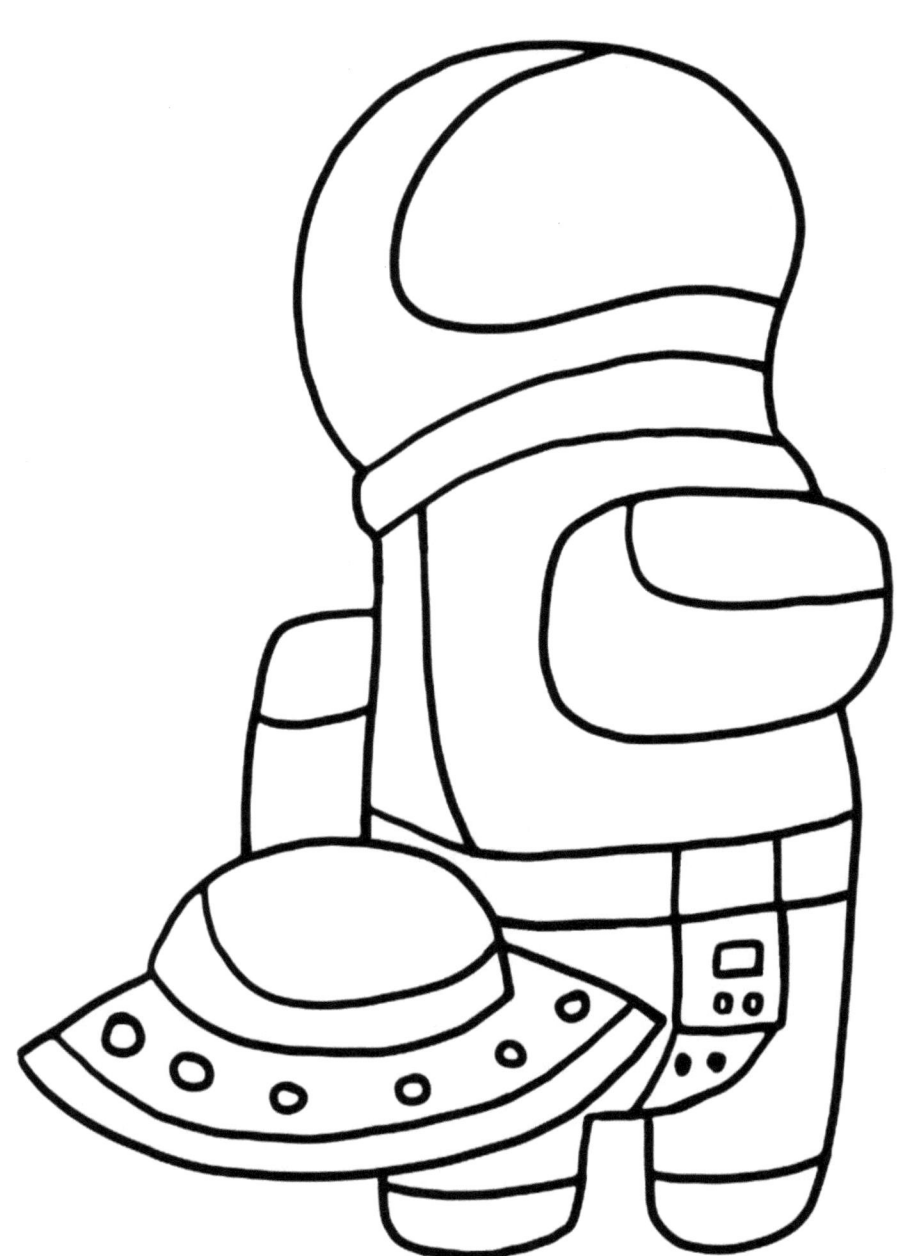

Step 1: We start with the outline of the hat, the body and of the ufo

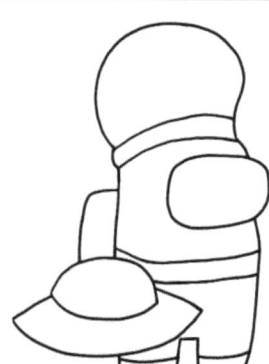

Step 2: We finish drawing the body, draw the oxygen tank, the visor and start with the clothes

Step 3: We complete the drawing with further details

Space for your drawing

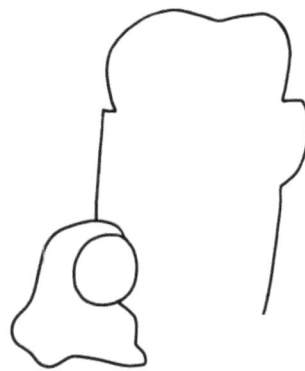

Step 1: We start with the outline of the mask, the body and the Brainslug

Step 2: We finish drawing the body, draw the oxygen tank, the visor and start with the clothes

Step 3: We complete the drawing with further details

Step 1: We start with the outline of the flower, the body and the Dog

Step 2: We finish drawing the body, draw the oxygen tank, the visor and start with the clothes

Step 3: We complete the drawing with further details

Space for your drawing

Step 1: We start with the outline of the hat, the body and the Brainslug

Step 2: We finish drawing the body, draw the oxygen tank, the visor and start with the clothes

Step 3: We complete the drawing with further details

Step 1: We start with the outline of the hat, the body and the Hamster

Step 2: We finish drawing the body, draw the oxygen tank, the visor and start with the clothes

Step 3: We complete the drawing with further details

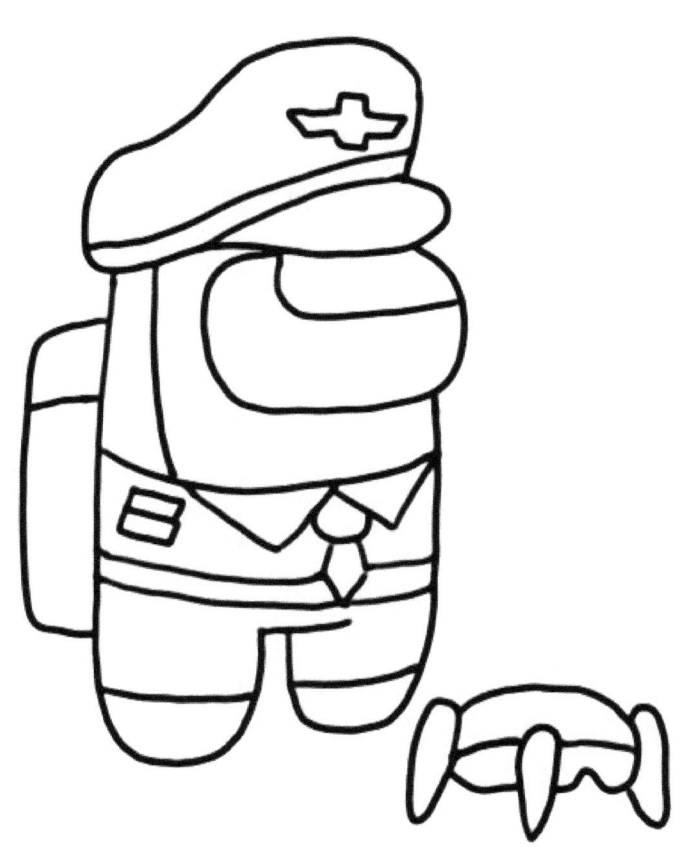

Space for your drawing

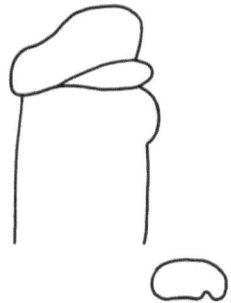

Step 1: We start with the outline of the hat, the body and the Bedcrab

Step 2: We finish drawing the body, draw the oxygen tank, the visor and start with the clothes

Step 3: We complete the drawing with further details

Space for your drawing

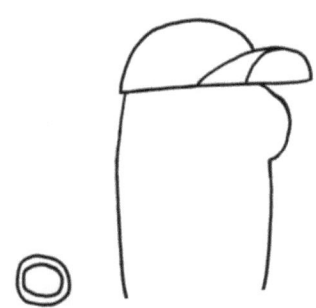

Step 1: We start with the outline of the hat, the body and the head of Henry

Step 2: We finish drawing the body, draw the oxygen tank, the visor and start with the clothes

Step 3: We complete the drawing with further details and Henry

Step 1: We start with the outline of the hat, the body and the Mini Crewmate

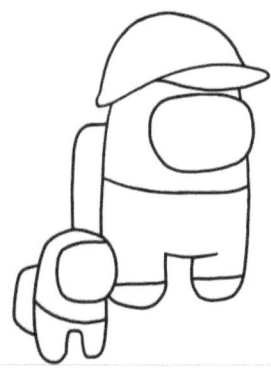

Step 2: We finish drawing the body, draw the oxygen tank, the visor and start with the clothes

Step 3: We complete the drawing with further details and the Mini Crewmate

Step 1: We start with the outline of the hat, the body and the Squig

Step 2: We finish drawing the body, draw the oxygen tank, the visor and start with the clothes

Step 3: We complete the drawing with further details and the Squig

Step 1: We start with the outline of the hat, the body and Ellie

Step 2: We finish drawing the body, draw the oxygen tank, the visor and start with the clothes

Step 3: We complete the drawing with further details and Ellie

SUPER
COLORING BOOK
for Ameng.us Fans

CREWMATES
COLORING BOOK
for Ameng.us Fans

The
SUPER
MAZE BOOK
for Ameng.us Fans

PASSWORD
LOGBOOK
for Ameng.us Fans

MATH
COLORING BOOK
for Ameng.us Fans

HOW TO DRAW
SKINS
for Ameng.us Fans

WORD SEARCH
PUZZLES
for Ameng.us Fans

SUPER
QUIZ
BOOK
for Ameng.us Fans

CARTOONS
MEMES and
JOKES
for Ameng.us Fans

WTF!

Notebook

Crewmate Notebook

Impostor
Notebook